NIST Special Publication 500-292

NIST Cloud Computing Reference Architecture

Recommendations of the National Institute of Standards and Technology

Fang Liu, Jin Tong, Jian Mao, Robert Bohn, John Messina, Lee Badger and Dawn Leaf

---

Information Techonology Laboratory

Cloud Computing Program
Information Technology Laboratory
National Institute of Standards and Technology
Gaithersburg, MD 20899-8930

September 2011

U.S. Department of Commerce

Rebecca M. Blank, Acting Secretary

National Institute of Standards and Technology

Patrick D. Gallagher, Under Secretary for Standards and Technology and Director

Reports on Computer Systems Technology

The Information Technology Laboratory (ITL) at the National Institute of Standards and Technology (NIST) promotes the U.S. economy and public welfare by providing technical leadership for the nation's measurement and standards infrastructure. ITL develops tests, test methods, reference data, proof of concept implementations, and technical analysis to advance the development and productive use of information technology. ITL's responsibilities include the development of technical, physical, administrative, and management standards and guidelines for the cost-effective security and privacy of sensitive unclassified information in Federal computer systems. This Special Publication 800-series reports on ITL's research, guidance, and outreach efforts in computer security and its collaborative activities with industry, government, and academic organizations.

National Institute of Standards and Technology Special Publication 500-292
Natl. Inst. Stand. Technol. Spec. Publ. 500-292, 35 pages (September 2011)

Acknowledgments

The authors, Fang Liu, Jin Tong, Jian Mao of Knowcean Consulting Inc. (services acquired via US NAVY SPAWAR contract), Robert Bohn, John Messina, Lee Badger, Dawn Leaf of the National Institute of Standards and Technology (NIST), wish to thank their colleagues who reviewed drafts of this document and contributed to its technical content. The authors gratefully acknowledge and appreciate the broad contributions from members of the NIST Cloud Computing Reference Architecture and Taxonomy Working Group and the Reference Architecture Analysis Team.

Trademark Information

All names are trademarks or registered trademarks of their respective owners.

Table of Contents

List of Figures

List of Tables

Executive Summary

The adoption of cloud computing into the US Government (USG) and its implementation depend upon a variety of technical and non-technical factors. A fundamental reference point, based on the NIST definition of Cloud Computing, is needed to describe an overall framework that can be used government-wide. This document presents the NIST Cloud Computing Reference Architecture (RA) and Taxonomy (Tax) that will accurately communicate the components and offerings of cloud computing. The guiding principles used to create the RA were 1) develop a vendor-neutral architecture that is consistent with the NIST definition and 2) develop a solution that does not stifle innovation by defining a prescribed technical solution. This solution will create a level playing field for industry to discuss and compare their cloud offerings with the US Government (USG). The resulting reference architecture and taxonomy for cloud computing was developed as an Actor/Role based model that lays out the central elements of cloud computing for Federal CIOs, Procurement Officials and IT Program Managers. The cloudscape is open and diversified and the accompanying taxonomy provides a means to describe it in an unambiguous manner. The RA is presented in two parts: a complete overview of the actors and their roles and the necessary architectural components for managing and providing cloud services such as service deployment, service orchestration, cloud service management, security and privacy. The Taxonomy is presented in its own section and appendices are dedicated to terms and definitions and examples of cloud services.

The *Overview* of the Reference Architecture describes five major actors with their roles & responsibilities using the newly developed Cloud Computing Taxonomy. The five major participating actors are the *Cloud Consumer, Cloud Provider, Cloud Broker, Cloud Auditor* and *Cloud Carrier*. These core individuals have key roles in the realm of cloud computing. For example, a Cloud Consumer is an individual or organization that acquires and uses cloud products and services. The purveyor of products and services is the Cloud Provider. Because of the possible service offerings (Software, Platform or Infrastructure) allowed for by the cloud provider, there will be a shift in the level of responsibilities for some aspects of the scope of control, security and configuration. The Cloud Broker acts as the intermediate between consumer and provider and will help consumers through the complexity of cloud service offerings and may also create value-added cloud services as well. The Cloud Auditor provides a valuable inherent function for the government by conducting the independent performance and security monitoring of cloud services. The Cloud Carrier is the organization who has the responsibility of transferring the data akin to the power distributor for the electric grid.

The *Architectural Components* of the Reference Architecture describes the important aspects of service deployment and service orchestration. The overall service management of the cloud is acknowledged as an important element in the scheme of the architecture. Business Support mechanisms are in place to recognize customer management issues like contracts, accounting and pricing and are vital to cloud computing. A discussion on Provisioning and Configuration points out the requirements for cloud systems to be available as needed, metered and have proper SLA management in place. Portability and Interoperability issues for data, systems and services are crucial factors facing consumers in adopting the cloud are also undertaken here. Consumers need confidence in moving their data and services across multiple cloud environments.

As a major architectural component of the cloud, Security and Privacy concerns need to be addressed and there needs to be a level of confidence and trust in order to create an atmosphere of acceptance in the cloud's ability to provide a trustworthy and reliable system. Security responsibilities, security consideration for different cloud service models and deployment models are also discussed.

1.   Introduction

1.1   Background

The National Institute of Standards and Technology (NIST) has been designated by Federal Chief Information Officer (CIO) Vivek Kundra with technical leadership for US government (USG) agency efforts related to the adoption and development of cloud computing standards. The goal is to accelerate the federal government's adoption of secure and effective cloud computing to reduce costs and improve services. The NIST strategy is to build a USG Cloud Computing Technology Roadmap which focuses on the highest priority USG cloud computing security, interoperability and portability requirements, and to lead efforts to develop standards and guidelines in close consultation and collaboration with standards bodies, the private sector, and other stakeholders.

The NIST cloud computing program was formally launched in November 2010 to support the federal government effort to incorporate cloud computing as a replacement for, or enhancement to, traditional information system and application models where appropriate. The NIST cloud computing program operates in coordination with other USG-wide cloud computing efforts (CIO Council/ISIMC, etc.) and is integrated with the Federal 25-point IT Management Reform Plan[1] and Federal Cloud Computing Strategy[2]. NIST has created the following working groups in order to provide a technically-oriented strategy and standards-based guidance for the federal cloud computing implementation effort:

> Cloud Computing Target Business Use Cases Working Group
> Cloud Computing Reference Architecture and Taxonomy Working Group
> Cloud Computing Standards Roadmap Working Group
> Cloud Computing SAJACC Working Group
> Cloud Computing Security Working Group

1.2   Objectives

The NIST cloud computing definition [1] is widely accepted as a valuable contribution toward providing a clear understanding of cloud computing technologies and cloud services. It provides a simple and unambiguous taxonomy of three service models available to cloud consumers: *cloud software as a service* (SaaS), *cloud platform as a service* (PaaS), and *cloud infrastructure as a service* (IaaS). It also summarizes four deployment models describing how the computing infrastructure that delivers these services can be shared: *private cloud, community cloud, public cloud,* and *hybrid cloud.* Finally, the NIST definition also provides a unifying view of five essential characteristics that all cloud services exhibit: *on-demand self-service, broad network access, resource pooling, rapid elasticity,* and *measured service.*

These services and their delivery are at the core of cloud computing. In the cloud computing model, the primary focus is a more economic method of providing higher quality and faster services at a lower cost to the users. In the traditional IT service delivery model, there is a large emphasis on procuring, maintaining and operating the necessary hardware and related infrastructure. The cloud computing model enables CIOs, IT project managers and procurement officials to direct their attention to innovative service creation for the customers.

In order to have successful service delivery, the USG needs to ensure the reliability in the delivery of products and processes. By ensuring durable and proper standards in place for cloud computing in security, data portability and service interoperability, the USG will have the additional confidence needed

---

[1]Office of Management and Budget, U.S. Chief Information Officer Vivek Kundra, "25 Point Implementation Plan to Reform Federal Information Technology Management", December 2010. http://www.cio.gov/documents/25-Point-Implementation-Plan-to-Reform-Federal%20IT.pdf

[2]Office of Management and Budget, U.S. Chief Information Officer Vivek Kundra, "Federal Cloud Computing Strategy", February 2011. http://www.cio.gov/documents/Federal-Cloud-Computing-Strategy.pdf

to move their applications into the cloud. The necessary standards will also promote an even playing field among cloud service providers and give the cloud service consumers a number of different options in the marketplace and the confidence that their data and applications will operate on any cloud.

Standards for cloud computing are the overall goal of the NIST cloud computing program; the logical step to take after the formation of the NIST cloud computing definition is to create an intermediate reference point from where one can frame the rest of the discussion about cloud computing and begin to identify sections in the reference architecture in which standards are either required, useful or optional. The NIST cloud computing reference architecture presented in this document is a logical extension to the NIST cloud computing definition. It is a generic high-level conceptual model that is an effective tool for discussing the requirements, structures, and operations of cloud computing. The model is not tied to any specific vendor products, services or reference implementation, nor does it define prescriptive solutions that inhibit innovation. It defines a set of actors, activities and functions that can be used in the process of developing cloud computing architectures, and relates to a companion cloud computing taxonomy. The reference architecture contains a set of views and descriptions that are the basis for discussing the characteristics, uses and standards for cloud computing. This actor/role based model is intended to serve the expectations of the stakeholders by allowing them to understand the overall view of roles and responsibilities in order to assess and assign risk.

The NIST cloud computing reference architecture focuses on the requirements of "what" cloud services provide, *not* a "how to" design solution and implementation. The reference architecture is intended to facilitate the understanding of the operational intricacies in cloud computing. It does not represent the system architecture of a specific cloud computing system; instead it is a tool for describing, discussing, and developing a system-specific architecture using a common framework of reference.

The design of the NIST cloud computing reference architecture serves the following objectives: to illustrate and understand the various cloud services in the context of an overall cloud computing conceptual model; to provide a technical reference to USG agencies and other consumers to understand, discuss, categorize and compare cloud services; and to facilitate the analysis of candidate standards for security, interoperability, and portability and reference implementations.

1.3 How This Report Was Produced

The NIST cloud computing reference architecture project team has surveyed and completed an initial analysis of existing cloud computing reference models proposed by cloud organizations, vendors and federal agencies. Based on available information, the project team developed a strawman model of architectural concepts. This effort has leveraged the collaborative process from the NIST cloud computing reference architecture and taxonomy working group that was active between November 2010 and April 2011. This process involves broad participation from the industry, academic, standards development organizations (SDOs), and private and public sector cloud adopters. The project team has iteratively revised the reference model by incorporating comments and feedback received from the working group. This document reports the first edition of the NIST cloud computing reference architecture and taxonomy.

1.4 Structure of This Report

The remainder of this document is organized as follows: Section 2 presents the overview of the NIST cloud computing reference architecture, lists the major actors and discusses the interactions among the actors. Section 3 drills down the details of the architectural components in the reference model. Section 4 depicts the associated taxonomy. The document also includes supporting materials in the appendices. Appendix A lists the terms and definitions appearing in the taxonomy. Appendix B includes some examples of cloud services. Appendix C and D list the acronyms and references used in the document, respectively.

2.   Cloud Computing Reference Architecture: An Overview

2.1   The Conceptual Reference Model

Figure 1 presents an overview of the NIST cloud computing reference architecture, which identifies the major actors, their activities and functions in cloud computing. The diagram depicts a generic high-level architecture and is intended to facilitate the understanding of the requirements, uses, characteristics and standards of cloud computing.

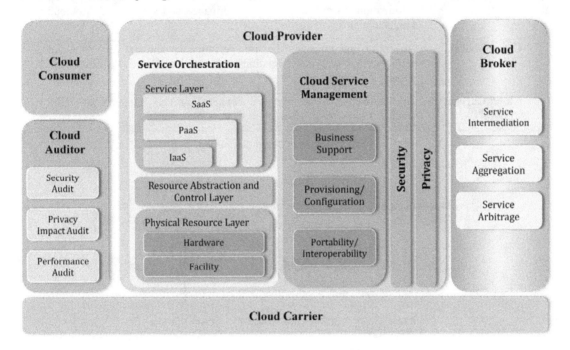

Figure 1: The Conceptual Reference Model

As shown in Figure 1, the NIST cloud computing reference architecture defines five major actors: *cloud consumer, cloud provider, cloud carrier, cloud auditor* and *cloud broker*. Each actor is an entity (a person or an organization) that participates in a transaction or process and/or performs tasks in cloud computing. Table 1 briefly lists the actors defined in the NIST cloud computing reference architecture. The general activities of the actors are discussed in the remainder of this section, while the details of the architectural elements are discussed in Section 3.

Figure 2 illustrates the interactions among the actors. A cloud consumer may request cloud services from a cloud provider directly or via a cloud broker. A cloud auditor conducts independent audits and may contact the others to collect necessary information. The details will be discussed in the following sections and presented in increasing level of details in successive diagrams.

Actor	Definition
Cloud Consumer	A person or organization that maintains a business relationship with, and uses service from, *Cloud Providers*.
Cloud Provider	A person, organization, or entity responsible for making a service available to interested parties.
Cloud Auditor	A party that can conduct independent assessment of cloud services, information system operations, performance and security of the cloud implementation.
Cloud Broker	An entity that manages the use, performance and delivery of cloud services, and negotiates relationships between *Cloud Providers* and *Cloud Consumers*.
Cloud Carrier	An intermediary that provides connectivity and transport of cloud services from *Cloud Providers* to *Cloud Consumers*.

Table 1: Actors in Cloud Computing

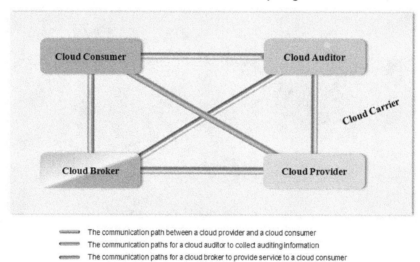

        The communication path between a cloud provider and a cloud consumer
        The communication paths for a cloud auditor to collect auditing information
        The communication paths for a cloud broker to provide service to a cloud consumer

Figure 2: Interactions between the Actors in Cloud Computing

- **Example Usage Scenario 1**: A cloud consumer may request service from a cloud broker instead of contacting a cloud provider directly. The cloud broker may create a new service by combining multiple services or by enhancing an existing service. In this example, the actual cloud providers are invisible to the cloud consumer and the cloud consumer interacts directly with the cloud broker.

Figure 3: Usage Scenario for Cloud Brokers

- **Example Usage Scenario 2**: Cloud carriers provide the connectivity and transport of cloud services from cloud providers to cloud consumers. As illustrated in Figure 4, a cloud provider participates in and arranges for two unique service level agreements (SLAs), one with a cloud carrier (e.g. SLA2) and one with a cloud consumer (e.g. SLA1). A cloud provider arranges service level agreements (SLAs) with a cloud carrier and may request dedicated and encrypted connections to ensure the cloud services are consumed at a consistent level according to the contractual obligations with the cloud consumers. In this case, the provider may specify its requirements on capability, flexibility and functionality in SLA2 in order to provide essential requirements in SLA1.

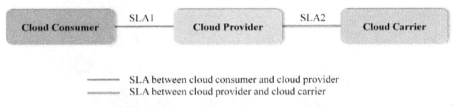

   SLA between cloud consumer and cloud provider
   SLA between cloud provider and cloud carrier

Figure 4: Usage Scenario for Cloud Carriers

- **Example Usage Scenario 3**: For a cloud service, a cloud auditor conducts independent assessments of the operation and security of the cloud service implementation. The audit may involve interactions with both the Cloud Consumer and the Cloud Provider.

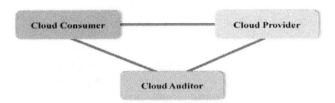

Figure 5: Usage Scenario for Cloud Auditors

2.2   Cloud Consumer

The cloud consumer is the principal stakeholder for the cloud computing service. A cloud consumer represents a person or organization that maintains a business relationship with, and uses the service from a cloud provider. A cloud consumer browses the service catalog from a cloud provider, requests the appropriate service, sets up service contracts with the cloud provider, and uses the service. The cloud consumer may be billed for the service provisioned, and needs to arrange payments accordingly.

Cloud consumers need SLAs to specify the technical performance requirements fulfilled by a cloud provider. SLAs can cover terms regarding the quality of service, security, remedies for performance failures. A cloud provider may also list in the SLAs a set of promises explicitly not made to consumers, i.e. limitations, and obligations that cloud consumers must accept. A cloud consumer can freely choose a cloud provider with better pricing and more favorable terms. Typically a cloud provider's pricing policy and SLAs are non-negotiable, unless the customer expects heavy usage and might be able to negotiate for better contracts. [2].

Depending on the services requested, the activities and usage scenarios can be different among cloud consumers. Figure 6 presents some example cloud services available to a cloud consumer (For details, see Appendix B: Examples of Cloud Services) [13].

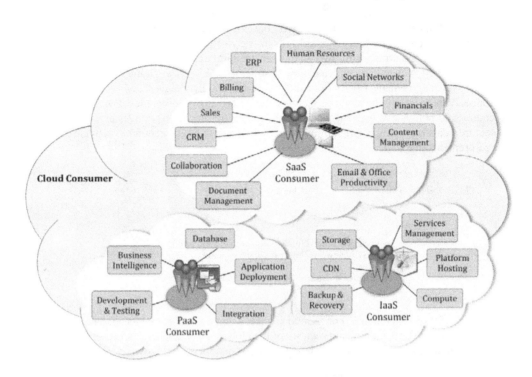

Figure 6: Example Services Available to a Cloud Consumer

SaaS applications in the cloud and made accessible via a network to the SaaS consumers. The consumers of SaaS can be organizations that provide their members with access to software applications, end users who directly use software applications, or software application administrators who configure applications for end users. SaaS consumers can be billed based on the number of end users, the time of use, the network bandwidth consumed, the amount of data stored or duration of stored data.

Cloud consumers of PaaS can employ the tools and execution resources provided by cloud providers to develop, test, deploy and manage the applications hosted in a cloud environment. PaaS consumers can be application developers who design and implement application software, application testers who run and test applications in cloud-based environments, application deployers who publish applications into the cloud, and application administrators who configure and monitor application performance on a platform. PaaS consumers can be billed according to, processing, database storage and network resources consumed by the PaaS application, and the duration of the platform usage.

Consumers of IaaS have access to virtual computers, network-accessible storage, network infrastructure components, and other fundamental computing resources on which they can deploy and run arbitrary software. The consumers of IaaS can be system developers, system administrators and IT managers who are interested in creating, installing, managing and monitoring services for IT infrastructure operations. IaaS consumers are provisioned with the capabilities to access these computing resources, and are billed according to the amount or duration of the resources consumed, such as CPU hours used by virtual computers, volume and duration of data stored, network bandwidth consumed, number of IP addresses used for certain intervals..

6

2.3   Cloud Provider

A cloud provider is a person, an organization; it is the entity responsible for making a service available to interested parties. A Cloud Provider acquires and manages the computing infrastructure required for providing the services, runs the cloud software that provides the services, and makes arrangement to deliver the cloud services to the Cloud Consumers through network access.

For Software as a Service, the cloud provider deploys, configures, maintains and updates the operation of the software applications on a cloud infrastructure so that the services are provisioned at the expected service levels to cloud consumers. The provider of SaaS assumes most of the responsibilities in managing and controlling the applications and the infrastructure, while the cloud consumers have limited administrative control of the applications.

For PaaS, the Cloud Provider manages the computing infrastructure for the platform and runs the cloud software that provides the components of the platform, such as runtime software execution stack, databases, and other middleware components. The PaaS Cloud Provider typically also supports the development, deployment and management process of the PaaS Cloud Consumer by providing tools such as integrated development environments (IDEs), development version of cloud software, software development kits (SDKs), deployment and management tools. The PaaS Cloud Consumer has control over the applications and possibly some the hosting environment settings, but has no or limited access to the infrastructure underlying the platform such as network, servers, operating systems (OS), or storage.

For IaaS, the Cloud Provider acquires the physical computing resources underlying the service, including the servers, networks, storage and hosting infrastructure. The Cloud Provider runs the cloud software necessary to makes computing resources available to the IaaS Cloud Consumer through a set of service interfaces and computing resource abstractions, such as virtual machines and virtual network interfaces. The IaaS Cloud Consumer in turn uses these computing resources, such as a virtual computer, for their fundamental computing needs Compared to SaaS and PaaS Cloud Consumers, an IaaS Cloud Consumer has access to more fundamental forms of computing resources and thus has more control over the more software components in an application stack, including the OS and network. The IaaS Cloud Provider, on the other hand, has control over the physical hardware and cloud software that makes the provisioning of these infrastructure services possible, for example, the physical servers, network equipments, storage devices, host OS and hypervisors for virtualization.

A Cloud Provider's activities can be described in five major areas, as shown in Figure 7, a cloud provider conducts its activities in the areas of *service deployment, service orchestration, cloud service management, security,* and *privacy.* The details are discussed in Section 3.

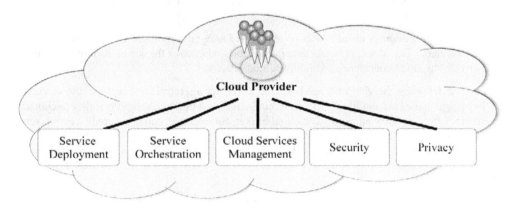

Figure 7: Cloud Provider - Major Activities

2.4   Cloud Auditor

A cloud auditor is a party that can perform an independent examination of cloud service controls with the intent to express an opinion thereon. Audits are performed to verify conformance to standards through review of objective evidence. A cloud auditor can evaluate the services provided by a cloud provider in terms of security controls, privacy impact, performance, etc.

Auditing is especially important for federal agencies as "agencies should include a contractual clause enabling third parties to assess security controls of cloud providers" [4] (*by Vivek Kundra, Federal Cloud Computing Strategy, Feb. 2011.*). Security controls [3] are the management, operational, and technical safeguards or countermeasures employed within an organizational information system to protect the confidentiality, integrity, and availability of the system and its information. For security auditing, a cloud auditor can make an assessment of the security controls in the information system to determine the extent to which the controls are implemented correctly, operating as intended, and producing the desired outcome with respect to the security requirements for the system. The security auditing should also include the verification of the compliance with regulation and security policy. For example, an auditor can be tasked with ensuring that the correct policies are applied to data retention according to relevant rules for the jurisdiction. The auditor may ensure that fixed content has not been modified and that the legal and business data archival requirements have been satisfied.

A privacy impact audit can help Federal agencies comply with applicable privacy laws and regulations governing an individual's privacy, and to ensure confidentiality, integrity, and availability of an individual's personal information at every stage of development and operation [5].

2.5   Cloud Broker

As cloud computing evolves, the integration of cloud services can be too complex for cloud consumers to manage. A cloud consumer may request cloud services from a cloud broker, instead of contacting a cloud provider directly. A cloud broker is an entity that manages the use, performance and delivery of cloud services and negotiates relationships between cloud providers and cloud consumers.

In general, a cloud broker can provide services in three categories [9]:

- *Service Intermediation*: A cloud broker enhances a given service by improving some specific capability and providing value-added services to cloud consumers. The improvement can be managing access to cloud services, identity management, performance reporting, enhanced security, etc.

- *Service Aggregation*: A cloud broker combines and integrates multiple services into one or more new services. The broker provides data integration and ensures the secure data movement between the cloud consumer and multiple cloud providers.

- *Service Arbitrage*: Service arbitrage is similar to service aggregation except that the services being aggregated are not fixed. Service arbitrage means a broker has the flexibility to choose services from multiple agencies. The cloud broker, for example, can use a credit-scoring service to measure and select an agency with the best score.

2.6   Cloud Carrier

A cloud carrier acts as an intermediary that provides connectivity and transport of cloud services between cloud consumers and cloud providers. Cloud carriers provide access to consumers through network, telecommunication and other access devices. For example, cloud consumers can obtain cloud services through network access devices, such as computers, laptops, mobile phones, mobile Internet devices (MIDs), etc [1]. The distribution of cloud services is normally provided by network and telecommunication carriers or a *transport agent* [8], where a transport agent refers to a business organization that provides physical transport of storage media such as high-capacity hard drives. Note that a cloud provider will set up SLAs with a cloud carrier to provide services consistent with the level of SLAs offered to cloud consumers, and may require the cloud carrier to provide dedicated and secure connections between cloud consumers and cloud providers.

2.7 Scope of Control between Provider and Consumer

The Cloud Provider and Cloud Consumer share the control of resources in a cloud system. As illustrated in Figure 8, different service models affect an organization's control over the computational resources and thus what can be done in a cloud system. The figure shows these differences using a classic software stack notation comprised of the application, middleware, and OS layers. This analysis of delineation of controls over the application stack helps understand the responsibilities of parties involved in managing the cloud application.

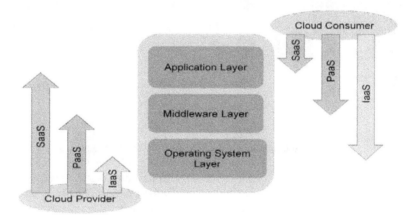

Figure 8: Scope of Controls between Provider and Consumer

- The application layer includes software applications targeted at end users or programs. The applications are used by SaaS consumers, or installed/managed/ maintained by PaaS consumers, IaaS consumers, and SaaS providers.

- The middleware layer provides software building blocks (e.g., libraries, database, and Java virtual machine) for developing application software in the cloud. The middleware is used by PaaS consumers, installed/managed/maintained by IaaS consumers or PaaS providers, and hidden from SaaS consumers.

- The OS layer includes operating system and drivers, and is hidden from SaaS consumers and PaaS consumers. An IaaS cloud allows one or multiple guest OS's to run virtualized on a single physical host. Generally, consumers have broad freedom to choose which OS to be hosted among all the OS's that could be supported by the cloud provider. The IaaS consumers should assume full responsibility for the guest OS's, while the IaaS provider controls the host OS.

3.   Cloud Computing Reference Architecture: Architectural Components

3.1   Service Deployment

As identified in the NIST cloud computing definition [1], a cloud infrastructure may be operated in one of the following deployment models: public cloud, private cloud, community cloud, or hybrid cloud. The differences are based on how exclusive the computing resources are made to a Cloud Consumer.

A public cloud is one in which the cloud infrastructure and computing resources are made available to the general public over a public network. A public cloud is owned by an organization selling cloud services, and serves a diverse pool of clients. Figure 9 presents a simple view of a public cloud and its customers.

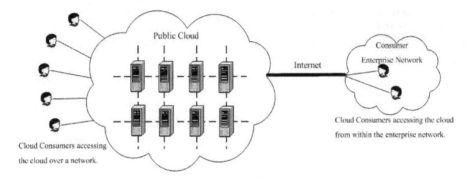

Figure 9: Public Cloud

A private cloud gives a single Cloud Consumer's organization the exclusive access to and usage of the infrastructure and computational resources. It may be managed either by the Cloud Consumer organization or by a third party, and may be hosted on the organization's premises (i.e. *on-site private clouds*) or outsourced to a hosting company (i.e. *outsourced private clouds*). Figure 10 and Figure 11 present an on-site private cloud and an outsourced private cloud, respectively.

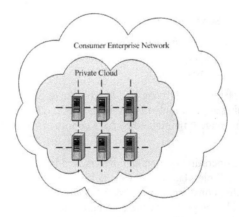

Figure 10: On-site Private Cloud

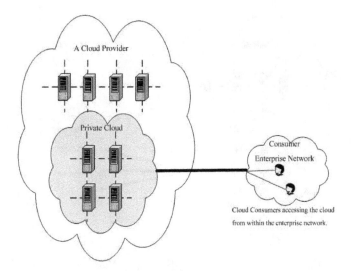

Figure 11: Out-sourced Private Cloud

A community cloud serves a group of Cloud Consumers which have shared concerns such as mission objectives, security, privacy and compliance policy, rather than serving a single organization as does a private cloud. Similar to private clouds, a community cloud may be managed by the organizations or by a third party, and may be implemented on customer premise (i.e. *on-site community cloud*) or outsourced to a hosting company (i.e. *outsourced community cloud*). Figure 12 depicts an on-site community cloud comprised of a number of participant organizations. A cloud consumer can access the local cloud resources, and also the resources of other participating organizations through the connections between the associated organizations. Figure 13 shows an outsourced community cloud, where the server side is outsourced to a hosting company. In this case, an outsourced community cloud builds its infrastructure off premise, and serves a set of organizations that request and consume cloud services.

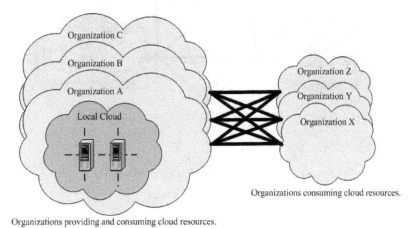

Figure 12: On-site Community Cloud

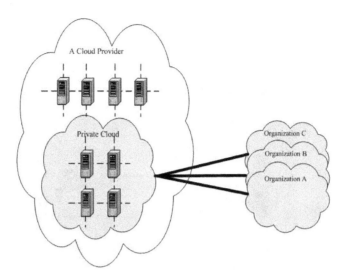

Figure 13: Outsourced Community Cloud

A hybrid cloud is a composition of two or more clouds (on-site private, on-site community, off-site private, off-site community or public) that remain as distinct entities but are bound together by standardized or proprietary technology that enables data and application portability. Figure 14 presents a simple view of a hybrid cloud that could be built with a set of clouds in the five deployment model variants.

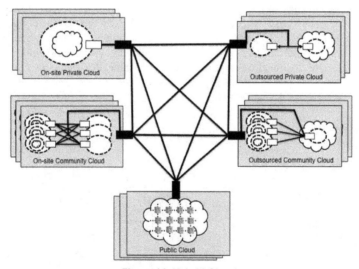

Figure 14: Hybrid Cloud

3.2   Service Orchestration

Service Orchestration refers to the composition of system components to support the Cloud Providers activities in arrangement, coordination and management of computing resources in order to provide cloud services to Cloud Consumers. Figure 15 shows a generic stack diagram of this composition that underlies the provisioning of cloud services.

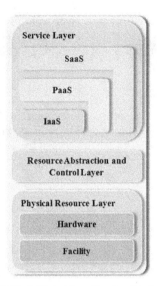

Figure 15: Cloud Provider - Service Orchestration

A three-layered model is used in this representation, representing the grouping of three types of system components Cloud Providers need to compose to deliver their services.

In the model shown in Figure 15, the top is the *service layer*, this is where Cloud Providers define interfaces for Cloud Consumers to access the computing services. Access interfaces of each of the three service models are provided in this layer. It is possible, though not necessary, that SaaS applications can be built on top of PaaS components and PaaS components can be built on top of IaaS components. The optional dependency relationships among SaaS, PaaS, and IaaS components are represented graphically as components stacking on each other; while the angling of the components represents that each of the service component can stand by itself. For example, a SaaS application can be implemented and hosted on virtual machines from an IaaS cloud or it can be implemented directly on top of cloud resources without using IaaS virtual machines.

The middle layer in the model is the *resource abstraction and control layer*. This layer contains the system components that Cloud Providers use to provide and manage access to the physical computing resources through software abstraction. Examples of *resource abstraction* components include software elements such as hypervisors, virtual machines, virtual data storage, and other computing resource abstractions. The resource abstraction needs to ensure efficient, secure, and reliable usage of the underlying physical resources. While virtual machine technology is commonly used at this layer, other means of providing the necessary software abstractions are also possible. The *control* aspect of this layer refers to the software components that are responsible for resource allocation, access control, and usage monitoring. This is the software fabric that ties together the numerous underlying physical resources and their software abstractions to enable resource pooling, dynamic allocation, and measured service. Various open source and proprietary cloud software are examples of this type of middleware.

The lowest layer in the stack is the *physical resource layer*, which includes all the physical computing resources. This layer includes hardware resources, such as computers (CPU and memory), networks (routers, firewalls, switches, network links and interfaces), storage components (hard disks) and other physical computing infrastructure elements. It also includes facility resources, such as heating, ventilation and air conditioning (HVAC), power, communications, and other aspects of the physical plant.

Following system architecture conventions, the horizontal positioning, i.e., the *layering*, in a model represents dependency relationships – the upper layer components are dependent on adjacent lower layer

13

to function. The resource abstraction and control layer exposes virtual cloud resources on top of the physical resource layer and supports the service layer where cloud services interfaces are exposed to Cloud Consumers, while Cloud Consumers do not have direct access to the physical resources.

3.3   Cloud Service Management

Cloud Service Management includes all of the service-related functions that are necessary for the management and operation of those services required by or proposed to cloud consumers. As illustrated in Figure 16, cloud service management can be described from the perspective of *business support, provisioning and configuration,* and from the perspective of *portability and interoperability* requirements.

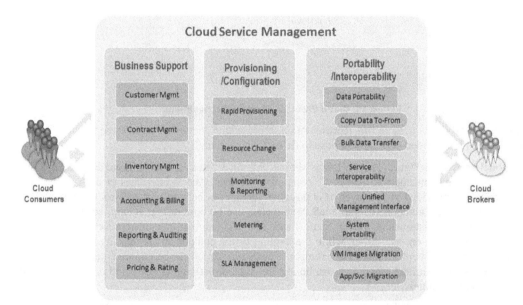

Figure 16: Cloud Provider - Cloud Service Management

3.3.1   Business Support

Business Support entails the set of business-related services dealing with clients and supporting processes. It includes the components used to run business operations that are client-facing.

- *Customer management*: Manage customer accounts, open/close/terminate accounts, manage user profiles, manage customer relationships by providing points-of-contact and resolving customer issues and problems, etc.

- *Contract management:* Manage service contracts, setup/negotiate/close/terminate contract, etc.

- *Inventory Management:* Set up and manage service catalogs, etc.

- *Accounting and Billing:* Manage customer billing information, send billing statements, process received payments, track invoices, etc.

- *Reporting and Auditing:* Monitor user operations, generate reports, etc.

- *Pricing and Rating:* Evaluate cloud services and determine prices, handle promotions and pricing rules based on a user's profile, etc.

3.3.2 Provisioning and Configuration

- *Rapid provisioning:* Automatically deploying cloud systems based on the requested service/resources/capabilities.

- *Resource changing:* Adjusting configuration/resource assignment for repairs, upgrades and joining new nodes into the cloud.

- *Monitoring and Reporting:* Discovering and monitoring virtual resources, monitoring cloud operations and events and generating performance reports.

- *Metering:* Providing a metering capability at some level of abstraction appropriate to the type of service (e.g., storage, processing, bandwidth, and active user accounts).

- *SLA management:* Encompassing the SLA contract definition (basic schema with the QoS parameters), SLA monitoring and SLA enforcement according to defined policies.

3.3.3 Portability and Interoperability

The proliferation of cloud computing promises cost savings in technology infrastructure and faster software upgrades. The US government, along with other potential cloud computing customers, has a strong interest in moving to the cloud. However, the adoption of cloud computing depends greatly on how the cloud can address users' concerns on security, portability and interoperability. This section briefly discusses the requirement for portability and interoperability, with security addressed in Section 3.4.

For portability, prospective customers are interested to know whether they can move their data or applications across multiple cloud environments at low cost and minimal disruption. From an interoperability perspective, users are concerned about the capability to communicate between or among multiple clouds.

Cloud providers should provide mechanisms to support *data portability, service interoperability*, and *system portability* [8]. Data portability is the ability of cloud consumers to copy data objects into or out of a cloud or to use a disk for bulk data transfer. Service interoperability is the ability of cloud consumers to use their data and services across multiple cloud providers with a unified management interface. System portability allows the migration of a fully-stopped virtual machine instance or a machine image from one provider to another provider, or migrate applications and services and their contents from one service provider to another.

It should be noted that various cloud service models may have different requirements in related with portability and interoperability [35]. For example, IaaS requires the ability to migrate the data and run the applications on a new cloud. Thus, it is necessary to capture virtual machine images and migrate to new cloud providers which may use different virtualization technologies. Any provider-specific extensions to the VM images need to be removed or recorded upon being ported. While for SaaS, the focus is on data portability, and thus it is essential to perform data extractions and backups in a standard format.

3.4 Security

It is critical to recognize that security is a cross-cutting aspect of the architecture that spans across all layers of the reference model, ranging from physical security to application security. Therefore, security in cloud computing architecture concerns is not solely under the purview of the Cloud Providers, but also

Cloud Consumers and other relevant actors. Cloud-based systems still need to address security requirements such as authentication, authorization, availability, confidentiality, identity management, integrity, audit, security monitoring, incident response, and security policy management. While these security requirements are not new, we discuss cloud specific perspectives to help discuss, analyze and implement security in a cloud system.

3.4.1 Cloud Service Model Perspectives

The three service models identified by the NIST cloud computing definition, i.e. SaaS, PaaS, and IaaS, present consumers with different types of service management operations and expose different entry points into cloud systems, which in turn also create different attacking surfaces for adversaries. Hence, it is important to consider the impact of cloud service models and their different issues in security design and implementation. For example, SaaS provides users with accessibility of cloud offerings using a network connection, normally over the Internet and through a Web browser. There has been an emphasis on Web browser security in SaaS cloud system security considerations [2]. Cloud Consumers of IaaS are provided with virtual machines (VMs) that are executed on hypervisors on the hosts, therefore, hypervisor security for achieving VM isolation has been studied extensively for IaaS Cloud Providers that use virtualization technologies.

3.4.2 Implications of Cloud Deployment Models

The variations of cloud deployment models discussed in section 3.1 have important security implication as well. One way to look at the security implications from the deployment model perspective is the differing level of exclusivity of tenants in a deployment model. A private cloud is dedicated to one consumer organization, where as a public cloud could have unpredictable tenants co-existing with each other, therefore, workload isolation is less of a security concern in a private cloud than in a public cloud. Another way to analyze the security impact of cloud deployment models is to use the concept of access boundaries as shown in [2]. For example, an on-site private cloud may or may not need additional boundary controllers at the cloud boundary when the private cloud is hosted on-site within the Cloud Consumer organization's network boundary, whereas an out-sourced private cloud tends to require the establishment of such perimeter protection at the boundary of the cloud.

3.4.3 Shared Security Responsibilities

As discussed in Section 2.7, the Cloud Provider and the Cloud Consumer have differing degrees of control over the computing resources in a cloud system. Compared to traditional IT systems, where one organization has control over the whole stack of computing resources and the entire life-cycle of the systems, Cloud Providers and Cloud Consumers collaboratively design, build, deploy, and operate cloud-based systems. The split of control means both parties now share the responsibilities in providing adequate protections to the cloud-based systems. Security is a shared responsibility. Security controls, i.e., measures used to provide protections, need to be analyzed to determine which party is in a better position to implement. This analysis needs to include considerations from a service model perspective, where different service models imply different degrees of control between Cloud Providers and Cloud Consumers. For example, account management controls for initial system privileged users in IaaS scenarios are typically performed by the IaaS Provider whereas application user account management for the application deployed in an IaaS environment is typically not the provider's responsibility.

3.5 Privacy

Cloud providers should protect the assured, proper, and consistent collection, processing, communication, use and disposition of personal information (PI) and personally identifiable information (PII) in the cloud [14].

According to the Federal CIO Council [5], one of the Federal government's key business imperatives is to ensure the privacy of the collected personally identifiable information. PII is the information that can be used to distinguish or trace an individual's identity, such as their name, social security number, biometric records, etc. alone, or when combined with other personal or identifying information that is linked or linkable to a specific individual, such as date and place of birth, mother's maiden name, etc [6]. Though cloud computing provides a flexible solution for shared resources, software and information, it also poses additional privacy challenges to consumers using the clouds.

4.   Cloud Taxonomy

Taxonomy is the science of categorization, or classification, of things based on a predefined system [22]. Typically, taxonomy contains a controlled vocabulary with a hierarchical tree-like structure.

Figure 17 presents the taxonomy associated with the cloud computing reference architecture discussed in this document. In the figure, a four-level taxonomy is presented to describe the key concepts about cloud computing.

- *Level 1: Role*, which indicates a set of obligations and behaviors as conceptualized by the associated actors in the context of cloud computing.
- *Level 2: Activity*, which entails the general behaviors or tasks associated to a specific role.
- *Level 3: Component*, which refer to the specific processes, actions, or tasks that must be performed to meet the objective of a specific activity.
- *Level 4: Sub-component*, which present a modular part of a component.

The companion controlled vocabulary is shown in Appendix A: Cloud Taxonomy Terms and Definitions.

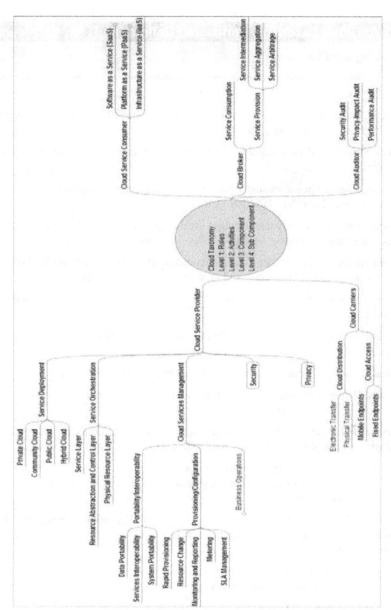

Figure 17: Cloud Taxonomy

Appendix A: Cloud Taxonomy Terms and Definitions

(Terms appearing in the Taxonomy)

==

First Level Terms:

1. Cloud Consumer - Person or organization that maintains a business relationship with, and uses service from, Cloud Service Providers.

2. Cloud Provider – Person, organization or entity responsible for making a service available to service consumers.

3. Cloud Carrier – The intermediary that provides connectivity and transport of cloud services between Cloud Providers and Cloud Consumers.

4. Cloud Broker – An entity that manages the use, performance and delivery of cloud services, and negotiates relationships between Cloud Providers and Cloud Consumers.

5. Cloud Auditor – A party that can conduct independent assessment of cloud services, information system operations, performance and security of the cloud implementation.

==

Second Level Terms:

6. Cloud Distribution – The process of transporting cloud data between Cloud Providers and Cloud Consumers.

7. Cloud Access – To make contact with or gain access to Cloud Services.

8. Service Deployment – All of the activities and organization needed to make a cloud service available

9. Service Orchestration - Refers to the arrangement, coordination and management of cloud infrastructure to provide different cloud services to meet IT and business requirements.

10. Cloud Service Management – Cloud Service Management includes all the service-related functions that are necessary for the management and operations of those services required by or proposed to customers.

11. Security – Refers to information security. 'information security' means protecting information and information systems from unauthorized access, use, disclosure, disruption, modification, or destruction in order to provide:

    (A) integrity, which means guarding against improper information modification or destruction, and includes ensuring information nonrepudiation and authenticity;

    (B) confidentiality, which means preserving authorized restrictions on access and disclosure, including means for protecting personal privacy and proprietary information;

    (C) availability, which means ensuring timely and reliable access to and use of information. (Source: [SOURCE: Title III of the E-Government Act, entitled the Federal Information Security Management Act of 2002 (FISMA)])

12. Privacy - Information privacy is the assured, proper, and consistent collection, processing, communication, use and disposition of disposition of personal information (PI) and personally-identifiable information (PII) throughout its life cycle. (Source: adapted from OASIS)

13. Software as a Service (SaaS) - The capability provided to the consumer is to use the provider's applications running on a cloud infrastructure. The applications are accessible from various client

devices through a thin client interface such as a web browser (e.g., web-based email). The consumer does not manage or control the underlying cloud infrastructure including network, servers, operating systems, storage, or even individual application capabilities, with the possible exception of limited user-specific application configuration settings. (Source: NIST CC Definition)

14. Platform as a Service (PaaS) - The capability provided to the consumer is to deploy onto the cloud infrastructure consumer-created or acquired applications created using programming languages and tools supported by the provider. The consumer does not manage or control the underlying cloud infrastructure including network, servers, operating systems, or storage, but has control over the deployed applications and possibly application hosting environment configurations. (Source: NIST CC Definition)

15. Infrastructure as a Service (IaaS) - The capability provided to the consumer is to provision processing, storage, networks, and other fundamental computing resources where the consumer is able to deploy and run arbitrary software, which can include operating systems and applications. The consumer does not manage or control the underlying cloud infrastructure but has control over operating systems, storage, deployed applications, and possibly limited control of select networking components (e.g., host firewalls). (Source: NIST CC Definition)

16. Service Consumption – A Cloud Broker in the act of using a Cloud Service.

17. Service Provision – A Cloud Broker in the act of providing a Cloud Service.

18. Security Audit - Systematic evaluation of a cloud system by measuring how well it conforms to a set of established security criteria.

19. Privacy-Impact Audit - Systematic evaluation of a cloud system by measuring how well it conforms to a set of established privacy-impact criteria.

20. Performance Audit - Systematic evaluation of a cloud system by measuring how well it conforms to a set of established performance criteria.

==

Third Level Terms:

21. Service Intermediation - An intermediation broker provides a service that directly enhances a given service delivered to one or more service consumers, essentially adding value on top of a given service to enhance some specific capability. (Source: Gartner)

22. Service Aggregation - An aggregation brokerage service combines multiple services into one or more new services. It will ensure that data is modeled across all component services and integrated as well as ensuring the movement and security of data between the service consumer and multiple providers. (Source: Gartner)

23. Service Arbitrage - Cloud service arbitrage is similar to cloud service aggregation. The difference between them is that the services being aggregated aren't fixed. Indeed the goal of arbitrage is to provide flexibility and opportunistic choices for the service aggregator, e.g., providing multiple e-mail services through one service provider or providing a credit-scoring service that checks multiple scoring agencies and selects the best score. (Source: Gartner)

24. Private Cloud - The cloud infrastructure is operated solely for an organization. It may be managed by the organization or a third party and may exist on premise or off premise. (Source: NIST CC Definition)

25. Community Cloud - The cloud infrastructure is shared by several organizations and supports a specific community that has shared concerns (e.g., mission, security requirements, policy, and

compliance considerations). It may be managed by the organizations or a third party and may exist on premise or off premise. (Source: NIST CC Definition)

26. Public Cloud - The cloud infrastructure is made available to the general public or a large industry group and is owned by an organization selling cloud services. (Source: NIST CC Definition)

27. Hybrid Cloud – The cloud infrastructure is a composition of two or more clouds (private, community, or public) that remain unique entities but are bound together by standardized or proprietary technology that enables data and application portability (e.g., cloud bursting for load-balancing between clouds). (Source: NIST CC Definition)

28. Service Layer - Defines the basic services provided by cloud providers

29. Physical Resource Layer - Includes all the physical resources used to provide cloud services, most notably, the hardware and the facility.

30. Resource Abstraction and Control Layer - Entails software elements, such as hypervisor, virtual machines, virtual data storage, and supporting software components, used to realize the infrastructure upon which a cloud service can be established.

31. Portability - The ability to transfer data from one system to another without being required to recreate or reenter data descriptions or to modify significantly the application being transported. 2. The ability of software or of a system to run on more than one type or size of computer under more than one operating system. *See* POSIX. 3. Of equipment, the quality of being able to function normally while being conveyed. [Source: Federal Standard 1037C]

32. Interoperability - The capability to communicate, to execute programs, or to transfer data among various functional units under specified conditions. [Source: American National Standard Dictionary of Information Technology (ANSDIT)]

33. Provisioning/Configuration - process of preparing and equipping a cloud to allow it to provide (new) services to its users

34. Mobile Endpoints - A physical device, often carried by the user that provided a man/machine interface to cloud services and applications. A Mobile Endpoint may use multiple methods and protocols to connect to cloud services and applications.

35. Fixed Endpoints - A physical device, fixed in its location that provided a man/machine interface to cloud services and applications. A fixed endpoint typically uses one method and protocol to connect to cloud services and applications.

===

Fourth Level Terms:

36. Data Portability – The ability to transfer data from one system to another without being required to recreate or reenter data descriptions or to modify significantly the application being transported. [Source: Federal Standard 1037C]

37. Service Interoperability - The capability to communicate, execute programs, or transfer data among various cloud services under specified conditions. [Source: modified from American National Standard Dictionary of Information Technology (ANSDIT)]

38. System Portability - The ability of a service to run on more than one type or size of cloud. [Source: modified from Federal Standard 1037C]

39. Rapid provisioning – Automatically deploying cloud system based on the requested service/resources/capabilities

40. Resource change – Adjust configuration/resource assignment for repairs, upgrades, and joining new nodes into the cloud

41. Monitoring and Reporting – Discover and monitor the virtual resources, monitor cloud operations and events, and generate performance reports.

42. Metering - Provide a measuring capability at some level of abstraction appropriate to the type of service (e.g, storage, processing, bandwidth, and active user accounts)

43. SLA management – Encompasses the SLA contract definition (basic schema with the quality of service parameters), SLA monitoring, and SLA enforcement, according to the defined policies.

Appendix B: Examples of Cloud Services

Some example cloud services available to a cloud consumer are listed below [13]:

- SaaS services:
  - *Email and Office Productivity*: Applications for email, word processing, spreadsheets, presentations, etc.
  - *Billing:* Application services to manage customer billing based on usage and subscriptions to products and services.
  - *Customer Relationship Management (CRM):* CRM applications that range from call center applications to sales force automation.
  - *Collaboration:* Tools that allow users to collaborate in workgroups, within enterprises, and across enterprises.
  - *Content Management:* Services for managing the production of and access to content for web-based applications.
  - *Document Management:* Applications for managing documents, enforcing document production workflows, and providing workspaces for groups or enterprises to find and access documents.
  - *Financials:* Applications for managing financial processes ranging from expense processing and invoicing to tax management.
  - *Human Resources:* Software for managing human resources functions within companies.
  - *Sales:* Applications that are specifically designed for sales functions such as pricing, commission tracking, etc.
  - *Social Networks:* Social software that establishes and maintains a connection among users that are tied in one or more specific types of interdependency.
  - *Enterprise Resource Planning (ERP):* Integrated computer-based system used to manage internal and external resources, including tangible assets, financial resources, materials, and human resources.
- PaaS Services:
  - *Business Intelligence:* Platforms for the creation of applications such as dashboards, reporting systems, and data analysis.
  - *Database:* Services offering scalable relational database solutions or scalable non-SQL datastores.
  - *Development and Testing:* Platforms for the development and testing cycles of application development, which expand and contract as needed.
  - *Integration:* Development platforms for building integration applications in the cloud and within the enterprise.
  - *Application Deployment*: Platforms suited for general purpose application development. These services provide databases, web application runtime environments, etc.
- IaaS Services:
  - *Backup and Recovery*: Services for backup and recovery of file systems and raw data stores on servers and desktop systems.
  - *Compute:* Server resources for running cloud-based systems that can be dynamically provisioned and configured as needed.

- o *Content Delivery Networks (CDNs):* CDNs store content and files to improve the performance and cost of delivering content for web-based systems.

- o *Services Management:* Services that manage cloud infrastructure platforms. These tools often provide features that cloud providers do not provide or specialize in managing certain application technologies.

- o *Storage:* Massively scalable storage capacity that can be used for applications, backups, archival, and file storage.

Appendix C: Acronyms

CDN	Content Delivery Networks
CIO	Chief Information Officer
CRM	Customer Relationship Management
ERP	Enterprise Resource Planning
HVAC	Heating, Ventilation and Air Conditioning
IaaS	Cloud Infrastructure as A Service
IT	Information Technology
MID	Mobile Internet Devices
NIST	National Institute of Standards and Technology
OS	Operating System
QoS	Quality of Service
SaaS	Cloud Software As A Service
SAJACC	Standards Acceleration to Jumpstart the Adoption of Cloud Computing
SDO	Standards Development Organization
SLA	Service Level Agreement
PaaS	Cloud Platform As A Service
PI	Personal Information
PII	Personally Identifiable Information
USG	US government

Appendix D: References

The lists below provide examples of resources that may be helpful.

[1]   NIST SP 800-145, "A NIST definition of cloud computing",
       http://csrc nist.gov/publications/drafts/800-145/Draft-SP-800-145_cloud-definition.pdf

[2]   NIST SP 800-146, "NIST Cloud Computing Synopsis and Recommendations",
       http://csrc nist.gov/publications/drafts/800-146/Draft-NIST-SP800-146.pdf

[3]   NIST SP 800-53, "Recommended Security Controls for Federal Information Systems and
       Organizations", http://csrc.nist.gov/publications/nistpubs/800-53-Rev3/sp800-53-rev3-
       final_updated-errata_05-01-2010.pdf

[4]   Federal Cloud Computing Strategy, http://www.cio.gov/documents/Federal-Cloud-Computing-
       Strategy.pdf

[5]   Chief Information Officers Council, "Privacy Recommendations for Cloud Computing",
       http://www.cio.gov/Documents/Privacy-Recommendations-Cloud-Computing-8-19-2010.docx

[6]   Office of Management and Budget, Memorandum 07-16,
       http://www.whitehouse.gov/sites/default/files/omb/memoranda/fy2007/m07-16.pdf

[7]   NIST SP 800-144, "Guidelines on Security and Privacy Issues in Public Cloud Computing",
       http://csrc nist.gov/publications/drafts/800-144/Draft-SP-800-144_cloud-computing.pdf

[8]   NIST Cloud Computing Use Cases, http://collaborate.nist.gov/twiki-cloud-
       computing/bin/view/CloudComputing/UseCaseCopyFromCloud

[9]   Gartner, "Gartner Says Cloud Consumers Need Brokerages to Unlock the Potential of Cloud
       Services", http://www.gartner.com/it/page.jsp?id=1064712.

[10]   IETF internet-draft, "Cloud Reference Framework", http://tools.ietf.org/html/draft-khasnabish-
       cloud-reference-framework-00

[11]   IBM, "Cloud Computing Reference Architecture v2.0",
       http://www.opengroup.org/cloudcomputing/doc.tpl?CALLER=documents.tpl&dcat=15&gdid=238
       40

[12]   GSA, "Cloud Computing Initiative Vision and Strategy Document (DRAFT)",
       http://info.apps.gov/sites/default/files/Cloud_Computing_Strategy_0.ppt

[13]   Cloud Taxonomy, http://cloudtaxonomy.opencrowd.com/

[14]   OASIS, the charter for the OASIS Privacy Management Reference Model Technical Committee,
       http://www.oasis-open.org/committees/pmrm/charter.php

[15]   Open Security Architecture (OSA), "Cloud Computing Patterns",
       http://www.opensecurityarchitecture.org/cms/library/patternlandscape/251-pattern-cloud-
       computing

[16]   Juniper Networks, "Cloud-ready Data Center Reference Architecture",
       www.juniper net/us/en/local/pdf/reference-architectures/8030001-en.pdf

[17]   Federal Information Security Management Act of 2002 (FISMA),
       http://csrc nist.gov/drivers/documents/FISMA-final.pdf

[18]   NIST IR-7756, DRAFT "CAESARS Framework Extension: An Enterprise Continuous Monitoring
       Technical Reference Architecture", http://csrc nist.gov/publications/drafts/nistir-7756/Draft-nistir-
       7756_feb2011.pdf

[19] NIST SP 800-61 Rev.1, "Computer Security Incident Handling Guide", http://csrc nist.gov/publications/nistpubs/800-61-rev1/SP800-61rev1.pdf

[20] Federal Standard 1037C, http://www.its.bldrdoc.gov/fs-1037/

[21] http://www.webopedia.com/TERM/T/taxonomy.html

[22] http://en.wikipedia.org/wiki/Enterprise_information_security_architecture

[23] http://en.wikipedia.org/wiki/Information_security

[24] http://en.wikipedia.org/wiki/Computer_security#Security_architecture

[25] The Open Group Architecture Framework (TOGAF), section 21.3, http://www.opengroup.org/architecture/togaf9-doc/arch/

[26] IBM, "Introducing the IBM Security Framework and IBM Security Blueprint to Realize Business-Driven Security", http://www redbooks.ibm.com/redpieces/pdfs/redp4528.pdf

[27] http://publib.boulder.ibm.com/infocenter/wmqv6/v6r0/index.jsp?topic=/com.ibm.mq.csqzas.doc/sy10280_.htm

[28] Cloud Computing Use Cases White Paper, http://groups.google.com/group/cloud-computing-use-cases

[29] DMTF, "Interoperable Clouds White Paper", http://www.dmtf.org/about/cloud-incubator/DSP_IS0101_1.0.0.pdf

[30] Cloud Security Alliance, "Security Guidance for Critical Areas of Focus In Cloud Computing V2.1", www.cloudsecurityalliance.org/csaguide.pdf

[31] CISCO, "Cisco Cloud Computing - Data Center Strategy, Architecture, and Solutions", http://www.cisco.com/web/strategy/docs/gov/CiscoCloudComputing_WP.pdf

[32] SNIA, "Cloud Storage for Cloud Computing", www.snia.org/cloud/CloudStorageForCloudComputing.pdf

[33] Stuart Charlton, "Cloud Computing and the Next Generation of Enterprise Architecture", http://www.slideshare.net/StuC/cloud-computing-and-the-nextgeneration-of-enterprise-architecture-cloud-computing-expo-2008-presentation

[34] Morrie Gasser, "Building a secure computer system", ISBN 0-442-23022-2, Van Nostrand Reinhold Co., 1988.

[35] "Security Guidance for Critical Areas of Focus in Cloud Computing", https://cloudsecurityalliance.org/wp-content/uploads/2011/07/csaguide.v2.1.pdf

www.ingramcontent.com/pod-product-compliance
Lightning Source LLC
Chambersburg PA
CBHW060513060326
40689CB00020B/4727